# BEING A CHRISTIAN

*What It Means and
How to Begin*

BY

WASHINGTON GLADDEN

 BOOKS FOR LIBRARIES PRESS
FREEPORT, NEW YORK

First Published 1876
Reprinted 1972

**Library of Congress Cataloging in Publication Data**

Gladden, Washington, 1836-1918
  Being a Christian.

  ([BCL/select bibliographies reprint series])
  Reprint of the 1876 ed.
  1.  Christian life.  I.  Title.
BV4501.G575  1972          248.4          72-4168
ISBN 0-8369-6880-8

# Preface

THIS little book will fall, I trust, into the hands of many who are not Christians. Some of them are not Christians simply because they do not want to be. They are not willing to give up their sins, and devote themselves to the unselfish service of Christ. But others of them do want to be Christians, only they do not know how to begin. Again and again they have tried to begin, and have always failed. They have heard that they must give their hearts to Christ, if they would be Christians; and they have knelt more than once, in secret, and said, just as honestly as they could,—

> "Here, Lord, I give myself away,
> 'Tis all that I can do,"—

waiting, then, for a light to shine down upon them, or for a burden to roll off, or for a flood of joy to fill their souls. Because nothing of the sort has ever happened to them, they have always sadly concluded that their consecration was not rightly made, that for some inscrutable reason God was not pleased to accept them; and their efforts to lead a Christian life have therefore been abandoned as often as they have been made.

Every faithful pastor knows that, in all our congregations, there are many such perplexed and discouraged seekers. These plain conversations are intended for them. No one will be made willing to be a Christian by reading this little book; but I hope that it may help those who are willing in finding the right way.

WASHINGTON GLADDEN

# Chapter I

## What is it to be a Christian?

THE ritualist is ready with his answer. "It is to be a member of the Christian Church," he tells you. "All who have been baptized with water in the name of the Father, the Son, and the Holy Ghost, are Christians."

In a certain formal sense this is true. All foreigners who have been naturalized are, before the law, Americans; and all human beings who have received baptism are, nominally at least, Christians. Baptism is the rite by which we are admitted to the visible Church, and those who have been baptized are members of the Church.

But we who have always lived in America are inclined to think that the simple act of taking out his naturalization papers will not make any man a good American. No man worthily bears that name, we say, who does not know something of the principles upon which this nation is founded, and who does not heartily devote himself to the maintenance of these principles in public and in private life. True Americans are not made by a process of law; it is by their sympathies, their choices, their heroic labors and sacrifices in behalf of their country, that they come to deserve the name. Just so the genuine Christian regards the mere act of baptism as giving one but a poor title to the Christian name. Paul said that the man was not a Jew who was one outwardly; that the mere rite of circumcision was nothing; that he was only a Jew who was one inwardly; and that the genuine circumcision was of the

5

heart, in the spirit and not in the letter. If Paul could say that about the Jewish Church, which was avowedly a ritualistic organization, surely it is safe to say the same thing about the Christian Church, which differs from the Jewish Church mainly in caring less for things ceremonial, and more for things spiritual; less for rites, and more for realities.

The definition of the ritualist, then, will never do. It describes the form of Christianity, but does not touch its substance. To say that a Christian is a person who has been baptized, is much the same as to say that a scholar is one who has received a diploma, or that a hero is a man who wears a blue uniform.

When the ritualist is done, up speaks the dogmatist. "To be a Christian," he says, "is to hold correct views of the plan of salvation. It is to have a realizing sense of the truth of certain sound doctrines concerning sin and the atonement." Faith, the dogmatist argues, is the condition of salvation; and faith, in his understanding of it, is a vivid perception of truth.

But faith, in this sense of the word, makes nobody a Christian. The devils are dogmatists. They also believe, after this fashion. They have a vivid perception of the truths against which they are all the while fighting. It is of great importance that we understand and believe the truth which relates to Christ and his kingdom; but the most unhesitating assent of the intellect to the whole of Hodge's Theology, or to all of Watson's Institutes, will make no man a Christian.

The sentimentalist also has his answer to our question. "To be a Christian," he says, "is to have certain delightful feelings of peace and joy and love. The impenitent person is one who feels that he is estranged from God: the Christian is one who feels that he is reconciled to God."

But our feelings, as everybody knows, are uncertain and even delusive guides. It is a notorious fact, that men often mistake the complacency which waits on good digestion for peace of conscience, and the excitement aroused by a dramatic appeal for joy in the Holy Ghost. Moreover, feeling is not the whole of life: when it serves its purposes, it is the glowing link which binds together thought and action. A feeling which originates in no definite thought, and results in no definite action, is good for nothing. Emotion for its own sake is poor stuff. Yet this is what the sentimentalist looks for, and labors to secure. When he has produced in himself or in others certain pleasurable states of feeling, his work is accomplished.

The ritualist, the dogmatist, and the sentimentalist represent three distinct classes of persons in every Christian community. Many of them are good Christians in practice, but their theories are unsound. Their lives are better than their ideas. It is only when they try to tell what it is to be a Christian, that they make mistakes; and those who seek to become Christians need to be put on their guard against these mistaken theories.

**To be a Christian is something more than to submit to certain rites, or to believe certain doctrines, or to experience certain emotions. What is it, then?**

To begin with, it seems clear that it must have something to do with Christ. "Christian" means literally, pertaining or belonging to Christ. When the word is applied to a man, it can only describe his personal relation to Jesus Christ; and it must mean that this relation is one of attachment and confidence.

7

*To be a Christian, then, is, in the first place, to believe on Jesus Christ.*

To believe *on* him, I say: not merely to believe *in* him, or to believe something *about* him, but to believe *on* him; and this, if I understand the New Testament, means, *to intrust your soul to him, and to trust in him for wisdom and strength and salvation.*

Of course you must believe in him, and must believe many things about him, in order to believe on him. If you think that no such person as Jesus Christ ever lived on the earth, and that the Gospels in which we read the story of his life and death are fabrications, you cannot believe on him. If you have come to the conclusion that he did probably live in Judæa nineteen hundred years ago, and that he uttered many of the words recorded in the Gospels, but that he was only a man; that, when he claimed to be more than a man, he was under a delusion; and that the narrative of his works and of his resurrection from the dead are the productions either of fraud or of fancy,—then, of course, you cannot believe *on* him. You cannot commit your soul to a mortal, who lived and died in a far-off land many centuries ago. To believe on him, you must at least believe that he said, "All power is given unto me in heaven and on earth," and that he spoke the truth when he said it. To believe on him, you must be persuaded, with his apostle, "that he is able also to save to the uttermost all who come unto God by him, seeing he ever liveth to make intercession for us." To believe on him, you must be convinced that he not only lived in Judæa in the days of Herod and Pilate, but that he lives to-day: that he not only knew Simon and John and Judas and Nicodemus, but that he knows you,—and that he is able not only to give you the help you want in trying to lead a better life, but to do for you exceeding abundantly above all that you ask or think.

There are those among us who do not believe so much as this about Christ. These words are not for them. I am sorry for their disbelief, and I do not admit that it is well founded; but I have not time now to argue with them these questions of fact. It is to those who do believe *in* Christ, and who believe all these things *about* him, that I speak, because they are the only ones who have any immediate interest in knowing what it is to be a Christian.

Believing on Christ is fundamental in the Christian life. The word "Christian" is used only three times in the New Testament; but the followers of Christ are often called believers, or those who believe. And this believing was, as we discover from the reading of the record, not a mere assent to the truths taught by Christ, nor a mere conviction that he was the Messiah, but a voluntary surrender of the heart and the life to his service, and an abiding trust in him as an ever-present Helper and Saviour. Faith, the New Testament most often calls it, and faith is the word which ought to describe it; but unfortunately this word has been so misused by the theologians, that it is almost sure to mislead those who hear it spoken. "Trust" is perhaps a better word for us to use. The Christian is one who intrusts himself to Christ, by the surrender of his will to Christ's direction, and of his life, to Christ's service; and who trusts in Christ's power to keep him from sin, to sustain him in sorrow, and to strengthen him for faithful and noble living.

In thus committing his soul, that is to say *himself,* to Christ, the believer establishes between himself and the Saviour a very close relation. The union which is thus formed is like that which exists between any two earthly friends; only Christ is so much wiser and stronger and more sympathizing than any human being can be, that we may come nearer to him than to any earthly friend, and confide in him more fully. The Christian comes at length to be identified with Christ in all his thoughts and wishes and purposes. The mind of Christ is his mind; the will of Christ is his will; the work of Christ is his work. At first he does not of course realize this so fully: he tries to trust and follow the Saviour, but his confidence often falters; this sense of oneness with Christ he does not always feel. The longer he serves his Master, however, the more complete this union with him becomes; the whole progress of his Christian life is toward a thorough identification of himself with his Lord, until at length he is able to say with Paul, "To live is Christ."

*The man who thus believes on Christ will also be a disciple of Christ.* The Christians of the early days were often called disciples. A disciple is a learner. Christ was a learner while he was on the earth; and he who has the mind of Christ will surely have a docile temper. He will not imagine that he knows everything; and to Christ, who is his teacher, he will constantly go for instruction in truth and in duty. The words that his Master spoke are written in the New Testament, and he will search those parables and conversations for hidden treasures of wisdom. Christ's word is law to him; when the Lord speaks, there is no more controversy.

And not only in the words of Christ does he find instruction, but in his acts as well. The Saviour's deeds were sermons not less than his words. The parables are miracles of speech, and the miracles are parables in act. By the Word of God all

10

things were made; and the Word that works in multiplying the loaves, and in healing the lepers, is one with the Word that speaks from the Mount of the Beatitudes.

And not only in the record of the Saviour's life does the disciple look for the truth that he needs to know. Christ promised, when he went away, that he would come again as the Spirit of Truth, and abide with his disciples, communicating directly to them enlightenment and wisdom. The Christian holds loving intercourse every day with the Spirit of the Lord. If there are questions of duty that he cannot solve, he asks for light, and is often sure that he receives it. He remembers that obedience is the condition of knowledge; that only those are certain to know of the doctrine, who are prompt to do the Master's will; and therefore he is careful always to be walking in the way of duty when he asks for light. But obedience is the only condition; and when it is supplied he knows that the divine Teacher is ready to impart to every trusting disciple the wisdom that is profitable to direct him, and the truth that will make him free.

*The man who believes on Christ will also be a follower of Christ.* He will not only be joined to Christ by a personal trust that identifies him with his Master; he will not only sit at the Saviour's feet as his disciple, and learn of him what is truth and what is duty: he will also arise, and follow Christ as his leader in the ways of fidelity and of sacrifice. He is not content with feeling as Christ felt, and with thinking as Christ thought: he wishes also to live as Christ lived. This, indeed, is the grand result of his belief and his discipleship. He trusts in Christ, and learns of him, in order that he may be able to follow him. It is not merely in view of death or of what comes after death, that he betakes himself to the Saviour: it is in

11

view of life, of its duties, its hardships, its temptations. The man who is a Christian merely that he may die securely and happily is a poor sort of Christian. He does not know the meaning of trust or of discipleship.

There are two paths in which the Christian follows Christ in this world,—paths which are always parallel, and which often merge into one,—the path of integrity, and the path of benevolence. In doing right and in doing good the Christian is a follower of Christ.

The righteousness of Christ is to the Christian not merely a shelter behind which he hides: it is an example which he imitates, and a living principle which by faith he makes his own. His own conscience tells him of a perfect truth, a perfect purity, a perfect goodness, which he ought to possess. He knows that these virtues are the most excellent possessions on earth, and he desires them above all things. In Christ he sees them incarnated and exemplified; and he therefore desires to "follow in His steps who did no sin, neither was guile found in his mouth."

The fact that Christianity means morality, aims at that, leads to that, results in that, is a fact of which scarcely enough account has been made, and which needs, especially in these days, to be made emphatic in any account of what Christianity is. Every one who thinks of becoming a Christian ought to understand at the outset, that being a Christian means telling the truth, dealing honestly in trade, governing the temper, sealing the lips against slander, keeping the mind free from evil thoughts and the life from unclean deeds; that he who has in him the good hope of salvation through Christ purifies himself even as Christ is pure. His name is called Jesus because he saves his people from their sins. He is not a Saviour to any man whom he does not save from sin. Any man who thinks he is a Christian, and who yet does wrong deliberately and persistently, deceives himself. He is not a Christian. The Christian may be overtaken in a fault; but when his fault is made plain to him he will repent of it and forsake it, making what reparation is in his power. But one who knowingly chooses to walk in the ways of sin, and who either brazenly justifies his iniquity, or falsely seeks to conceal it, has no reason to think that he is a Christian at all.

The man who goes to the bank, and tells the cashier that his assets are twenty thousand dollars when he knows that they are not really five thousand, and that his liabilities are five thousand dollars when he knows that they are twenty thousand, and who gets a note discounted there on the strength of the statement, and goes off with the money, and presently fails, paying twenty-five cents on the dollar, and never afterward repenting of his sin, or trying to restore the money of which he has plundered the bank, is not a Christian. No man who walks in that crooked road can be said to be a follower of Christ.

The man who contracts to build a house for you of sound and well-seasoned material, in a workmanlike manner, and then slips in timbers that he knows will shrink, and crack your walls; and water-pipes that he knows will burst, and flood your ceilings,—the man who habitually practises dishonesty of this sort is not a Christian. The man who sells you food, with the understanding that it is pure, when he knows it to be adulterated, who makes this the method of his business, is not a Christian. The woman who is addicted to putting in circulation or keeping in circulation evil tales which she does not

13

know to be true is not a Christian. Bearing false witness against your neighbors is not following Christ.

I do not mean that no one is a Christian who ever commits sins of this nature; the best Christians, I repeat, are sometimes led into temptation: but in sitting at Christ's feet, and learning of him, they are sure to be convinced of their sins, and then they make haste to repent of them, and forsake them. *The deliberate and habitual practice of any form of dishonesty or immorality is impossible to one who follows Christ.*

But the Christian is not satisfied with merely keeping to the right, with giving to all their just dues. Christ went a great deal further than that, and so must the man who follows him. If the Lord from heaven had been content with giving to all of us our just dues, it would not have been so well with us as it is to-day. He not only does justly: he loves mercy; and so shall we if we learn of him and follow him.

To do good to all men as we have opportunity; to do good to those who have no claim upon us but the claim of human brotherhood; to show kindness to the unthankful and the evil,— this is part of what is meant by following Jesus Christ. He went about doing good; and those who follow him must walk in the same ways of beneficence. Mrs. Barbauld's hymn tells us how the Christian feels and acts in the midst of the sorrow and suffering that fill the world:

> "Blest is the man whose softening heart
>     Feels all another's pain;
>   To whom the supplicating eye
>     Was never raised in vain;
>
> "Whose breast expands with generous warmth,
>     A stranger's woes to feel,

And bleeds in pity o'er the wound
    He wants the power to heal.

"To gentle offices of love
    His feet are never slow:
He views, through mercy's melting eye,
    A brother in a foe."

This bountiful and self-denying charity is one of the cardinal elements in the genuine Christian life; and the man who does not possess it and practise it has no reason to call himself a Christian. No matter how honest he may be: if he lives all for himself; if, with ability to help and comfort and bless his fellow-men, he does nothing or next to nothing for their welfare, and does what he does surlily and grudgingly, finding no pleasure in ministering to the woes and brightening the lives of his fellow-men,—that mind cannot be in him that was in Christ Jesus, nor can he be said to be in any true sense a follower of the Man of Nazareth.

I have been thus explicit in showing you what is involved in following Christ, because it is important that all who enter upon the Christian life do so understandingly. It ought to be clear, that the Christian life is the life of Christ, copied just as fairly as we are able to copy it; that it means always integrity and benevolence; and that they who are not made upright and generous by their religion are not Christians at all.

These words are spoken in the hope that they will reach the ears of some who, with the full knowledge of what is involved in following Christ, will want to follow him; will want to follow him just because the paths in which he leads his disciples are the paths of integrity and benevolence. They are spoken with the earnest expectation that some one who hears them will say, "That is just what I want to be. I want to be upright and pure and good. I want to cease to do evil, and to learn to do well. There is no comfort in doing wrong. I have tried it, and I know. Every time I am guilty of deceit or impurity or gluttony, of any kind of animalism or devilism, I feel degraded in my own eyes. I know, too, that all that is good within me is weakened by every such act of sin, and that if I keep on in this way I shall be helpless by and by, even to choose the better life. Moreover I know that there is happiness in doing right and in doing good; for I have found the most perfect enjoyment that I ever have known in walking in those ways. I want to keep in them henceforth and always. I know that they are the only right paths for men to walk in; and, since they are the paths into which Christ leads his own, I want to follow him. To stand erect in the right road, and go on in it to the end of life; to do that which is right in the sight of God; to live blamelessly and beneficently, conquering sin, and crowning the lives of my fellows with loving kindness,—this is reward enough in itself. I ask no more. I should be ashamed of myself if there was not in this thought the very highest motive to the Christian life. But one who knows tells me that Christ is able not only to keep me from falling here, but to present me faultless before the presence of his Father with exceeding joy. What that reward may be, I dare not stop to think now; but, if I follow on to know the Lord, I shall find out in his good time."

Believing on Christ, learning of Christ, following Christ,—this is what it is to be a Christian. You must believe on him that you may learn of him; you must learn of him that you may follow him. But believing is nothing, and learning is less than nothing, if they do not result in faithful following.

## Chapter II

### Why should I be a Christian?

THAT is a question which I am almost ashamed to spend any breath in answering. To one who lives in a Christian land, and who knows, either by travel or reading, any thing of the lands that are not Christian, there would seem to be no need of stating the reasons for being a Christian. But, unfortunately, many of those who have been breathing the air of our religion and subsisting upon its benefits all their lives, have become so utterly sophisticated in their notions about it, that it is necessary to stop and argue with them concerning its value as a personal possession.

Certain reasons for beginning the Christian life readily suggest themselves to those who are in the habit of going to church. One is, that there are terrible retributions for sin in the world to come, and that believing on Christ is the only way of escaping from them. Another is, that there is infinite blessedness in the world to come, and that believing on Christ is the only way of gaining it. Still another reason often urged is this: that we shall be happier in this world if we are engaged in Christ's service. "You had better become a Christian if you want to enjoy yourself. I never knew what happiness was till I experienced religion." Living a Christian life is by some persons always called "enjoying religion." Heaven is to them pre-eminently "a land of pure delight" (if the hymn read *"mere* delight," it would express their view about as clearly) ; and the life that leads to heaven gives some foretaste of the immortal joy.

"The hill of Zion yields
    A thousand sacred sweets
Before we reach the heavenly fields,
    Or walk the golden streets."

The promise of entering into this joy, on earth as well as in heaven, is, with some persons, the strongest reason for beginning the Christian life.

These three motives—the fear of hell, the desire of enjoyment in this life, and the hope of blessedness in the life to come—are often urged upon you; and I have no wish to ignore them or to belittle them. That sin does entail everlasting woe upon those who continue in it, is a truth of which I have no doubt. That Christ does deliver those who trust in him, from eternal suffering, I fully believe. That they who follow Christ will not only reach at length a land of pure delight, but that they will find enjoyment all along the way, I am very sure. I do not dwell upon these considerations, because you are already familiar with them, and because there are other motives higher and deeper and mightier than these, which are not so often urged, and upon which the emphasis of our exhortations ought always to be put.

But you may wonder whether it is possible that any higher or worthier motives could be presented to your minds, when we urge you to accept of salvation through Christ. "Can there be a worse evil," you ask, "than an eternity of suffering? Can there be a greater good than an eternity of joy?"

To all of which I answer, Yes: there is a worse evil than eternal suffering; there is a greater good than eternal enjoyment. A million years of suffering is less to be dreaded than

18

one year of sinning. An eternity of enjoyment is less to be craved than a mortal lifetime of purity and holiness. Not suffering, but sin, is the primal evil in this universe. Suffering is the consequence of sin; but the cause is worse than the consequence. Suffering may be honorable: sin can never be otherwise than shameful and detestable.

Not enjoyment, but rectitude, is the chief good, both in this life and in the life which is to come. Enjoyment flows from rectitude; but the fountain is higher and purer than the stream. Enjoyment is often an end unworthy to be sought. Rectitude is always to be desired above all things.

The reason for being a Christian which ought, then, to have the most weight with every human being, is this: that Christ promises to help those who trust in him and follow him, in overcoming sin, and in winning virtue. That, indeed, is the very thing that he came into this world to do. Many of the consequences of sin we must suffer so long as we remain in this world; but from sin itself he is ready to make us free if we will only believe on him. If deliverance from suffering had been the main reason of his coming, he would have provided a way of escape from that in this life, instead of which he often employs the discipline of suffering as a means of purifying us from sin; exactly reversing our own inclination, which leads us to commit sin in order to relieve ourselves from suffering. Does not this show us which of these evils he regards as the greater?

While, therefore, it is my duty to tell you that sin and pain always go together, that endless sin means endless misery, and that the way of holiness is the way of happiness, it is also my business to show you—and I know that your consciences are on my side when I say it—that, if sin brought no pain with it, it ought above all things to be hated; that, if holiness brought no happiness with it, it ought before all things to be craved.

Is it not so? Think of the evil with which your own life is infested. Your sins are not all alike: some of you are beset and crippled by one form of wrong-doing, and some by another; but the long catalogue of evil practices contains more than one kind of iniquity to which you will sorrowfully confess that you are more or less addicted.

Perhaps you are the bond-slave of appetite, and your spirit is often dragged in the mire of sensual indulgence, and soiled almost beyond hope of cleansing. And, when you think of these excesses into which your bodily cravings have some-times led you, are you not filled with a nameless horror, a deep and bitter shame? Saying nothing about the punishment threatened against those who defile their bodies that were made to be temples of the living God, is not the sin that merits the punishment something unspeakably heinous? And it is you who ought to be wearing the white robes of purity and honor; you who are not a brother of the beasts, but one of the sons of God; you who have all your life been instructed in purity and temperance, and pointed to the shining way in which God leads his own,—it is you who are suffering yourself to be debauched and corrupted by these swinish indulgences. Is it not a horrible offence, a dreadful degradation?

It may be that your worst fault is an evil temper. You are terribly passionate. On slight provocation, the baleful fires of anger light up your cheeks, and flash out of your eyes. When the fit is on you, you are sure to say and do unjust

20

and injurious things; things which you cannot defend in your cooler moments, but which you are yet too proud to confess. Or, it may be that your temper is sullen rather than fiery, and that you often wrong yourself, and inflict great discomfort upon others, by carrying a surly brow and a moody manner into places where you ought to be buoyant or cheerful. Or, it may be that you are a born tyrant, and that you are inclined to make your will the law of the little realm of which you are the ruler, driving ruthlessly over the rights and the preferences of your subjects. It is a mean passion, this lust of power; and it makes any man feel mean who indulges it.

It may be that envy or jealousy—twin demons—are the evil spirits to which your breast often affords a shelter. Like that truculent monarch, King Saul, who "eyed David" because the people applauded his courage, who hated him because good men loved him, who wanted to kill him because he behaved himself wisely and prospered in his wise behavior, you often find yourself cherishing grudges against your neighbors because they are more successful or more popular than you are. For their prosperity or their good fortune you bear them a secret ill-will. If King Saul ever had a sane moment, he must have despised himself for giving way to this detestable spirit. And so do you, I think, when you are conscious of having harbored the same devil in your own heart.

Or, perhaps you have been guilty of injustice in your dealings with your neighbors. The cursed greed of gain has led you to outwit and ensnare them, to overreach them in bargaining, to trample on their rights, and defraud them of their possessions. You have spoiled the innocent and the unwary, you have heaped up your own fortunes on the ruins of other men's estates; you have stolen the hearthstones of the poor

21

to build the walls of your own houses. You think sometimes of the injustice and treachery of which you have been guilty; and, while you cannot bring yourself to disgorge your gains, you cannot help hating yourself for the practice of the bad arts by which you have gotten them.

Or, it may be that you have a habit of untruth. Cowardice, or avarice, or love of applause, often leads you to say the thing that is not. You reflect upon these sayings afterward; and when conscience rises up and says, "That was a lie: you are a liar," your heart sinks and your flesh creeps in the presence of the dread accuser. Oh, it is a horrible thing to lie, to break the fair bond of confidence by which society is held together, to turn the very light that is in you into darkness!

And, what is worse, these sins of unchastity, of intemperance, of gluttony, of evil temper, of tyranny, of envy and jealousy, of injustice and extortion, of falsehood and dishonor, or whatever else your besetting faults may be, are sins which you commit deliberately and persistently. More than once you have yielded to these temptations. Against the protest of your consciences, against the warnings of God's law, against the pleadings of his Spirit, you persevere in these sinful practices. You know that you are walking in the broad road, yet you keep right on in it. These sins come to have a horrible fascination over you. Dreadful as they are, you do not shake them off. Their toils are bound more and more firmly round you every day; you yield to them with less and less compunction; you find yourself drawn down lower and lower by the gravitation of iniquity.

But I will not believe that any of you have reached this lower deep of moral degradation. I believe that all of you feel the

22

terror and the misery of sin, and desire to be freed from it. With some of you this feeling is more intense than with others, but there are few who do not share it. And every one who knows what this feeling is can perfectly understand the one grand reason for being a Christian. For it is to this very feeling that Christ addresses his gospel. To all who labor in these toils of sin, and cannot escape from them; to all who are heavy laden with iniquity, and are sinking under the load,— he comes offering deliverance and salvation. "If we confess our sins, he is faithful and just to forgive us our sins, and *to cleanse us from all unrighteousness.*" Not only to wipe off the old score, but to purge the heart from the evil desires out of which our transgressions flow. "And ye know," urges the beloved disciple, *"that he was manifested to take away our sins; and in him is no sin."* It is just what the blessed angel told his mother: his name foreshadows his work; he is called Jesus, Saviour, because he saves his people from their sins. "For the grace of God that bringeth salvation hath appeared to all men, teaching us that, denying ungodliness and worldly lusts, we should live soberly, righteously, and godly in this present world; looking for that blessed hope and the glorious appearing of the great God and our Saviour Jesus Christ, who gave himself for us that he might purify unto himself a peculiar people, zealous of good works."

Can any better news than that be told to any man who knows what an accursed thing sin is? Can any better hope be implanted in any human heart than the hope of triumph over the inbred evil? Is it possible to offer any stronger reason why men should intrust themselves to Jesus Christ, and begin to follow him, than this: "Jesus Christ is able and willing to deliver you from your sins"?

23

To be clean and pure; to have the body in perfect subjection, so that no clamorous appetite should ever drown the voice of reason; to be able to keep the temper in perfect equipoise, so that no blasts of passion and no clouds of sullenness should ever disturb the mind's clear sky; to be generous and charitable always, hoping all things, believing all things, enduring all things; to be upright and honorable; to be true in speech and true in act; to be without fear and without reproach, and with a conscience void of offence before God and men,—oh, what a hope! what a promise! what a destiny! But this is the goal toward which Jesus Christ is leading all those who follow him. Alas, that so many should be content to follow him as Peter did, a great way off!

Of some such particular sins and faults as I have mentioned, every man's conscience reproves him. But are not these sins and faults symptoms of an organic disease, for which a constitutional remedy is needed? Is not your bottom trouble, my friend, your estrangement from God? Is not this the reason of all your sins? You will deny that you hate him; but do you not sometimes find yourself distrusting him, shrinking away from him, banishing from your minds the thought of him? Your sins have separated between you and your God, and your separation from God has plunged you into sin. There is a terible reaction here, under which every unbelieving soul is driven further and further from goodness and from God. And sometimes, when you are not thinking of any particular sins, the sense of this unfriendliness toward God, the consciousness of your own unfilial feeling, distresses you beyond measure. This, more than anything else, is the cause of that strange unrest which often troubles you. You never can be quite at peace with yourself, my friend, until you are at peace with God. And one reason for being a Christian is found in the fact that God in Christ was and is reconciling men unto himself. They who commit their souls to him are made partakers of his peace. To them who are in Christ Jesus there is no condemnation, and there ought to be no feeling of condemnation: they are able to say "Abba Father," and to draw near to God with confidence in his forgiving grace.

What I have said already implies that Christ not only offers us the negative good of salvation from sin, but also the positive good of the enlargement and re-enforcement of our whole nature. "He that hath the Son hath life," new life, fuller life, fresher and stronger life. "I am come that ye might have life, and that ye might have it more abundantly." That is his own testimony. "As many as received him, to them gave he *power to become the sons of God.*" There is no other gift like that. There is no culture that can confer upon a man power like that. In delivering us from the bondage of corruption he leads us forth into the glorious liberty of the sons of God.

The personal friendship of Jesus Christ is in itself a strong reason for being a Christian. Suppose that some great and good man, the greatest and the best that you can think of, should offer you the freedom of his house, and kindly urge you to count yourself among his chosen friends, and to spend as much of your time as you could with him; if you knew that the offer was sincere, and that your acceptance of it would really give him pleasure, would you hesitate long in making known to him your gratitude for the favor, and your purpose to avail yourself as often as possible of his hospitality, and his friendly offices? Is not the friendship of Christ worth more to you than the friendship of any man could be? Is there not more of stimulus, more of strength, to be gained by communion with

25

him, than any mortal could give you? And is there not in the promise of knowing him who said to his disciples, "Henceforth I call you not servants, but friends," one strong reason for entering upon the Christian life?

We are often in perplexity and doubt; and Christ gives, to those who trust him, wisdom for their daily choices. He is the Light that lighteth every man that cometh into the world.

We are often in trouble; and he is the Comforter who comes to bind up our broken hearts, and wipe away our tears. No sympathy is so deep as his, no comfort so sweet, no support so strong. Are there not reasons here that approve themselves to your experience?

There is another consideration which ought, it seems to me, to have weight with some of you. That is the fact that the life to which Christ leads those who follow him is not only a life of purity and integrity, but also a life of heroic service, of self-denying love. It is the very noblest life of which it is possible for man to conceive. He who pleased not himself, but freely gave himself for all; he who lived to lighten the burdens and soothe the sorrows of men,—is a Master whom any man might be glad and proud to serve. If your souls do not kindle with ardor at the thought of following Him who went about doing good, and sharing the joy that was set before him when he entered upon his life of sacrifice, I am sorry for you.

I can speak of but one reason more why you should be a Christian; and that is the reason of personal gratitude. Surely Christ has done something for you. You may not be entirely clear what it is; but you know that you have been all your life a sharer in the blessings that he brought from heaven. You know that the whole world is a different world to live in to-day from what it would have been if Christ had not lived and died. You know that your relations to God, your thoughts of God, your opportunities of knowledge and of joy in this life and in the life to come, have been greatly changed by Christ's suffering love. You know that there is no other being in the universe, to whom you owe so much. Is there not in this fact a reason why you should love him and serve him? So thought that noble Catholic missionary, Francis Xavier, whose hymn you ought to know:

> "I love thee, O my God! but not
>     For what I hope thereby;
>   Nor yet because who love thee not
>     Must die eternally.
> I love thee, O my God! and still
>     I ever will love thee,
>   Solely because my God thou art,
>     Who first hast lovèd me.
>
> "For me to lowest depths of woe
>     Thou didst thyself abase;
>   For me didst bear the cross, the shame,
>     And manifold disgrace;
>   For me didst suffer pains unknown,
>     Blood sweat and agony,
>   Yea, death itself—all, all for me,
>     For me, thine enemy.
>
> "Then, shall I not, O Saviour mine!
>     Shall I not love thee well?
>   Not with the hope of winning heaven,
>     Nor of escaping hell;

27

Not with the hope of earning aught,
  Not seeking a reward;
But freely, freely as thyself
  Hast lovèd me, O Lord!"

Need I mention any more reasons why you ought to be a Christian? Let us go back over the way by which we have come, and mark the steps that have brought us hither:

Christ is the Redeemer of the world; it is to his love that we owe our lives, and all our blessings.

He is the Friend on whose arm we may lean in every time of trouble.

He is the Guide whose unfailing wisdom will serve us in moments when the ways are dark.

He is the Source and Inspiration of all worthy and beautiful life.

He is the Reconciler, who brings us near to God.

He is the Saviour from sin.

The sin from which he saves us is preparing our eternal ruin; and the life to which he leads us is crowned with everlasting joy.

Are there not reasons enough, and strong enough, why you should be a Christian?

Now tell me one good reason why you are not a Christian.

You know that there is not one.

## Chapter III

## How shall I become a Christian?

ONE who knows what it is to be a Christian may be supposed to know what he must do to become a Christian. Becoming is only beginning to be. Nothing can be plainer than that; yet no subject was ever more befogged. Almost everybody has an impression that one who wishes to become a Christian must go through some elaborate and mysterious mental process.

For this confusion, our controversial theology is largely to blame. There has been so much dispute about the plan of salvation, and the terms of salvation, that many persons have been greatly troubled to know just what salvation is, and how it is to be obtained. To them, it seems to be a bewildering maze of unintelligible and even contradictory theories. There appear to be a great many steps to take, and there is often a degree of uncertainty as to which step should be taken first. "Must repentance precede faith, or faith repentance? Should I pray before I repent and believe, or must I repent and believe before I can pray?" How often such questions as these are heard!

Here, for example, is a letter I received through the post-office:

"Do you think the Lord ever answers the prayers of a sinner? Please tell us what you think about it some evening, and oblige

AN INQUIRER."

Now, that is the question of an honest mind, I make no doubt; and the answer to it may dispel a little of the fog which hangs about the entrance to the Christian life. Certainly, my unknown friend, the Lord does answer the prayers of sinners. If he did not, there would be small hope for me. Every person who commits sin is a sinner; and I never yet knew any person who did not commit sin. If God did not answer the prayers of sinners, he would answer no prayers at all. You want to know, then, what is meant by that verse in the Bible which says, "The prayer of the wicked is an abomination to the Lord." That verse is not in the Bible. Here is what you are trying to remember, and you will see that you have remembered it very imperfectly:—"He that turneth away his ear from hearing the law, even his prayer shall be an abomination." One who wilfully refuses to obey God will not be answered when he prays. One who deliberately continues in the practice of any sin mocks God when he prays. But the sincere soul that is conscious of sin, and desires to be free from it, is the very one whose prayer the Lord hears soonest, and answers first.

But possibly your question means, "Does the Lord answer the prayers of one who is not a Christian?" Surely he does; else how could the unconverted person become a Christian? It is in answer to the prayer for pardon and help that the grace of God is given, by which the Christian life is begun. Did you ever read the parable of the lost sheep? Does it not tell you that the Son of man is come to seek and save them that are lost? And, if *he seeks them* when they are straying, is it not likely that he will answer their call when they seek him? He makes his sun to shine upon the evil and the good, and sends his rain upon the just and the unjust. Is it likely that one who bestows his temporal mercies upon sinners as freely as upon saints would bestow the better gifts of his grace only upon saints, and refuse them to sinners even when they ask for them? No, my friend: God always gives most readily to those who are in the greatest need. That is his nature. No creature in the universe needs his grace so much as the sinner; and, though he never forces his love upon those who do not want it, the moment that any earnest heart sends up to him a cry for help in overcoming sin, that moment his help comes down, quicker than the sunlight leaps from the sky to fill the cup of the modest flower that lifts itself up toward heaven.

Do but consider, my friend. Suppose that some poor creature who had hitherto been living a wretched life should come to me, and say, "Help me! I want to break off my bad habits; I want to lead a purer life; I want to find better associates and better employment. I want to be a Christian if I can." Do you suppose that I would turn away from him, saying, "No: you don't belong to my church; you have no claim upon me; I can do nothing for you"? Don't you think it a good deal more likely that I would make him understand very quickly, that the work of helping men in his condition is the very work above all others that I want to do, the very work which this church of Christ that I serve is organized to do? Could any minister of the gospel of Christ reply in any other way? And do you not think that Christ himself is at least as good as any of his ministers, as ready to hear and answer prayer?

It is very important at the outset, that we get rid of this strange confusion about the prayers of sinners. There is more joy in heaven over one sinner that repenteth than over ninety and nine just persons who need no repentance. It was the

31

publican, and not the Pharisee, who went down to his house justified.

The impression prevails, that the inquirer must pass through some remarkable transitional experience before he can pray aright, and before any of his acts will be acceptable to God. Going through that transitional experience is what he calls becoming a Christian. He does not know what it is, but he has some sort of vague notion about how he shall feel when he is going through it; and, until he feels in that way, he will not believe that he is a Christian. As nearly as I can find out when I talk with these persons, they suppose, that, in passing from the state of sin to the state of holiness, they will be as helpless and as ignorant as the poor little kitten that is put into a basket or a bag, and carried from one town to another; and that they will feel very much as the kitten feels when it is released in its new home, and looks about in a dazed way upon scenes which it never saw before. Until this mysterious passage is made, no act which properly belongs to the Christian life can without presumption be performed by them.

No delusion could be worse than this. Becoming a Christian is just beginning to be a Christian; nothing more, nothing less. You become a student by beginning to study: there is no other way. You become an artist by beginning to draw or to carve. You become a machinist by going into a machine-shop, and beginning to work at the trade of a machinist. And you become a Christian by choosing the Christian life, and beginning immediately to do the duties which belong to it.

What it is to be a Christian, we have seen already. It is to believe on Christ, to learn of him, and to follow him. To become a Christian is simply *to begin doing these things.*

## How shall I become a Christian?

It is to commit yourself to his care, and to consecrate yourself to his service at once and forever.

It is to ask him to show you what is truth, and what is duty.

It is to walk right on, then, in the light that he gives you, following his example and keeping his commandments.

If any thing more than this is included in becoming a Christian, I do not know what it is.

There is no ordeal to pass through; there is no mysterious process of initiation; there is no oracle to visit, no labyrinth to thread, no arcanum to discover: all you have to do is to *"commit the keeping of your soul to Him in well doing,"* and, seeking his guidance, to follow on in the way he leads.

Read the New Testament, and learn how men became Christians in the days of Christ.

"And Jesus, walking by the Sea of Galilee, saw two brethren, Simon called Peter, and Andrew his brother, casting a net into the sea; for they were fishers. And he saith unto them, Follow me, and I will make you fishers of men. And they straightway left their nets, and followed him. And going on from thence he saw two other brethren, James the son of Zebedee, and John his brother, in a ship with Zebedee their father, mending their nets; and he called them. And they immediately left the ship and their father and followed him." At another time "Jesus saw a man named Matthew sitting at the receipt of custom, and he saith unto him, Follow me. And he arose and followed him."

Here is no elaborate and toilsome process. It is the simplest thing in the world. The Master calls; the disciple follows. That is the beginning and the end of it.

But some will say, "These men were not converted at this time; for the Holy Spirit that regenerates the heart was not yet given. They were not converted until the day of Pentecost." Oh, absurd deduction of a machine-made theology! As if any man who surrenders himself to Christ as his Leader and his Lord were not in that act converted! How can any man call Jesus Lord but by the Holy Ghost? What a preposterous notion it is, that these disciples who gave their lives to the Saviour, who took his yoke upon them, and learned of him, who followed him whithersoever he went, and faithfully obeyed his orders, were not Christians! I only wish that all the members of our churches nowadays were just such Christians. If every one of you would set about becoming Christians in the same way, the number of the disciples would multiply very fast. Trust me, my friends, when you take Christ for your Master and Lord, when your life is knit with his by a living faith, the power that cleanses the heart and sanctifies the soul is not very far from you.

"But what about repentance?" somebody is asking. "Nothing has been said about repentance. Is not that one of the things to be done in becoming a Christian?" Certainly; and the things you have been told to do involve repentance. To repent is to forsake sin; and that is just what the man does who sets out to follow Christ. All the sorrow that is required to constitute repentance is just enough to lead us to forsake sin. And no man will ever begin to follow the sinless Saviour till he is tired of sin, and willing to forsake it.

"But is it not necessary," somebody else is asking, "that some feeling should accompany this step? Can I start right off in the Christian life in this cool and deliberate manner?" Undoubtedly you can. That was the way that James and John and Simon and Andrew started. We do not learn that they put on sackcloth, and waited in Capernaum, bewailing their sins, and going through with a regular course of conviction before they followed Christ. There is no account of their refusing to stir until some powerful impulse seized them, and pushed them on in the way by which Christ had gone. "Straightway," when Jesus called them, "they left their nets, and followed him." You know a great deal more about him than they knew then. You need his wisdom and grace at least as much as they did; and there is no reason why you should not respond just as promptly as they did.

When any duty is to be done, it is fortunate for you to feel like doing it; but, if you do not feel like it, that is no reason for not doing it. Suppose that a note of yours is due to-morrow at the bank; and a friend who happens to know it, and who thinks that you have forgotten about it, hurries in just before the close of banking hours, to remind you of it; to whom you reply, "Oh, yes: I know it; and I suppose I ought to go down and pay it. The money is here in my safe, and I have been thinking of it all day; but, for some reason, I don't feel moved to do it at all. I know it will injure my credit very much to have the note protested; and I suppose that I ought to feel deeply anxious about it; but somehow I don't. Do you think it would be right for me, feeling as I do, to go down to the bank, and pay the note?" What would your friend think if he heard you talk in that way? Yet that is exactly the way in which some of you do talk about an obligation which is certainly not less plain and not less urgent.

Some one rings your bell, and tells you that a man has fainted upon your doorstep, and is lying there in the cold in danger of perishing. "Ah, yes," you say: "poor fellow! I saw him lying there half an hour ago. He ought to be taken care of, doubtless; and, if I only felt moved to do it, I would bring him in, and try to resuscitate him. But I find no such impulse in my heart; and it would surely be hypocrisy for me to manifest an interest in him which I do not feel."

How would the plea of a want of feeling serve in a case like that? Believe me, my friend, it serves no better to excuse your hesitation in beginning the Christian life. Lack of inclination, want of impulse, is a poor apology for failure in the performance of plain duty. If you know that sin is disgraceful and ruinous; if you believe that Christ is able and ready to save you from sin, then the plea that you do not feel like availing yourself of his aid is both silly and shameful.

Sometimes the fact that a person feels disinclined to a course of conduct is the very reason why he ought to enter upon it. One who has taken an overdose of opium does not feel like keeping his body in active exercise. Yet that is just what he must do to save his life. If he is permitted to lie down and go to sleep, he will never awaken. Perhaps you may be in a similar condition.

"But this account of what must be done to become a Christian is very different," you say, "from the accounts that I have often heard. The experiences of many Christians, as they have been related in my hearing, show that they have passed into the service of Christ through long and painful conflicts, through agonies of contrition, through gulfs of dark despair." That is true, but it does not follow that their experience was one that anybody ought to imitate. If they were so headstrong that they struggled long before they would submit to the Master's yoke, if they were so proud that they could not without a painful strife surrender their souls to his keeping, that is no reason why you, too, should be proud and headstrong.

When I was a farmer's boy I remember once, on a stormy night, trying to get the sheep of which I had the care into a safe shelter. Most of them seemed ready enough to go in, but there was one who would not. I tried to call him in; but he stood outside stamping his feet and shaking his head in a very defiant fashion. I tried to drive him in; but he would turn suddenly from the narrow entrance, and leap past me, and then stand at a little distance, and bleat, as if he were a deeply injured animal. At last, by masterly strategy, I succeeded in getting him in, and fastening the door behind him. Once in, he seemed to enjoy the fold as much as any other member of the flock. But I presume that, if you could have got him to relate his experience, he would have told you it was a terrible thing to go into a sheepfold, that it was only accomplished after many struggles and doubts and fears.

There are a great many sheep in Christ's fold who have had much the same sort of a time in getting in, and some of them think that their way is the only right way of entering. I do not think so. It is not becoming, when Christ's call is heard, for any of us to devote our time to fruitless lamentations over our past misdeeds, or to any scenic exhibitions of our own perverseness. The only thing for us to do is to arise and follow. We shall most clearly show our sorrow for past neglect by prompt obedience and faithful living in the present.

These sentimental struggles of the soul before conversion are frequently of the nature of penances. They often grow out of the idea that suffering is a good thing in itself, that God is pleased to see us torture ourselves awhile before he consents

37

to forgive us. The Roman Catholic Bible reads, "Do penance, for the kingdom of heaven is at hand." Our Bible says, "Repent ye, for the kingdom of heaven is at hand." The two commands are utterly unlike. Doing penance is using your sins as scourges with which to lacerate yourself. Repenting is turning away from your sins, and forsaking them. That is what the man does who, like Matthew or the Ethiopian eunuch, instantly surrenders himself to the call of Christ. That is not what the man does who waits, before obeying the call, to put himself through an ordeal of contrition. He does penance, but he does not repent.

No: there are no long stages of preparation through which you must pass; all things are now ready; there is nothing to hinder you from becoming a Christian this very hour. And, if any of you have been trying to make yourself better until you are weary and discouraged in the work, all you have to do is to put it into stronger hands. By this I do not mean that you shall abandon the work of trying to do right, but that you shall give the direction of it to a Master workman, and you yourself become his industrious and faithful servant.

One day, in the City of New York, as I was walking up Third Avenue, I saw a little boy standing near the Bible House, by the side of a huge bundle of stationer's stores. He had been tugging it for some distance, and he was pretty well tired out. As I approached him, he looked up into my face, and said modestly, "Please, sir, can you tell me how I could get this bundle up to Twenty-first Street?" It was an appeal that I could not refuse; so thrusting my walking-stick through the cords of the package, and giving him the longest end of it, we lifted the bundle, and trudged on together till we reached the stationer's shop.

38

### How shall I become a Christian?

Now there were several other things that little boy might have done. He might have gone away, and left his bundle in the street, that would have been unfaithfulness to the trust reposed in him. He might have asked me to help him carry it a block or two, then he would have been but a little better off. He might have asked me to help him, insisting that I should give him the entire management of the job, if he had, I presume I should have been disinclined to help him. Or he might have requested me to carry it for him, refusing to lend a hand himself: then I should surely have left him to get it home the best way he could. But what he did do seemed to me the most sensible thing that such a little boy with such a big bundle, so far from home, could have done; and the grateful "Thank you, sir," with which he parted from me at the door of his shop, amply paid me for my labor and delay.

Now, it seems to me, my friends, that some of you are in that little boy's condition. You have a heavy load to carry, and you are a long way from home. You have a charge to keep, a labor to perform, which often seems too hard for you. To live purely and blamelessly, to subdue your appetites and passions,—this is your task. To carry with an even hand the heavy obligations of life up the narrow way of rectitude.—this is your burden. You have become pretty thoroughly convinced that you can never bear it alone. But what will you do? Will you abandon your burden in despair? All you have, that is worth saving, is bound in it. A Wayfaring Man is passing by. Perhaps he will help you. Among all the throngs of passengers, he is the only one whose eye is cast upon you. Will you speak to him? What will you say to him? Will you ask him to help you carry it a little way? That is what many people are inclined to do. They are willing to have a little temporary help from Christ; but they are not willing to take his yoke upon them with a pledge to bear it while they live. This casual grace, if you could obtain it, is not what you want.

Will you ask him to help you, but insist on having all the control of the work yourself? Which is the wiser,—you, or he?

Will you ask him to carry it for you, and then yourself refuse to do what he bids you? That prayer he will not hear. He helps those who help themselves,—none others. The burden of guilt, of anxiety, of fear,—that he will carry for you, the whole of it. His forgiveness will be so prompt and free, that it will lift that load in a moment from your heart. But there will still be duties to do, and responsibilities to bear, of which you must not expect to be relieved. Christ did not come to deliver you from labor: he came to help you in the performance of labors that were too heavy for you. His grace supplements, it does not supplant, your own activity. When you hear the sound of a going in the tops of the mulberry-trees, you are not to lie down in the shade: you are to bestir yourself.

Will you, then, do just what the little boy did,—ask him humbly to help you, making no conditions or suggestions or reservations whatever? Will you tell him frankly, that you cannot carry your load, and that you need help? Will you suffer him to help you in his own way, and be glad and thankful if he will only take you under his care, and direct the whole course of your life for you?

That, my friends, is the only right way, the only sensible way. The wayfaring man, Christ Jesus, has helped many and many a tired traveller home with burdens quite as heavy as yours. Often and often he goes up and down this thoroughfare of life in search of just such overladen pilgrims; and his voice is sounding forth above all the babble of the busy tongues and the clatter of the busy wheels, saying,—

"Come unto me, all ye that labor and are heavy laden, and I will give you rest.

"Take my yoke upon you, and learn of me; for I am meek and lowly in heart: and ye shall find rest unto your souls.

"For my yoke is easy, and my burden is light."

## Chapter IV

### How shall I know whether I am a Christian, or not?

FOR many good people this is a hard question. Within the churches are a multitude of sincere souls whose deepest thought finds expression in John Newton's homely quatrain,—

> " 'Tis a point I long to know,
>    Oft it causes anxious thought:
> Do I love the Lord, or no?
> Am I his, or am I not?"

This uncertainty greatly distresses them. They fear that they are in a false position, and they are continually searching their own lives for evidences that they are true children of God.

Outside the churches are many in the same perplexity. They have tried to become Christians, but they are not at all sure that they have succeeded. If they should be asked whether they are Christians or not, they would probably answer in the negative; yet they feel certain that they have done everything that they can do to secure the forgiveness of their sins, and the favor of their heavenly Father; and they do not see why they are not accepted of him.

I have no doubt that many of these are Christians. In all our congregations, and in many of our Christian families, are persons who are true disciples and followers of Christ, but who have never been able to reach this assurance, because they have always been looking for it in wrong places. They are defrauding themselves of a good hope. They are shutting themselves, by this distrust, out of joy which belongs to them, and out of work which they ought to be doing. I wish that I might make the matter so plain to them that they would enter at once into their duty and their reward.

Is this question necessarily a difficult one? Must the answer to it be involved in obscurity? It does not seem to us, when we begin to think about it, that it ought to be. If God calls men into his service, and tells them that their well-being in this life and in the life to come depends upon their heeding his call, it is surely not reasonable to suppose that he would make it difficult for them to know whether they have obeyed it or not. Suppose that an epidemic is destroying the lives of hundreds of people, and that a physician discovers a sure preventive. In itself it is something very simple; but his prescription which he gives to the public is so abstruse and complicated in its phraseology, that nobody can be clear whether he has followed it or not. Consequently all those who have attempted to protect themselves against the disease are left with the distressing apprehension that they may have made some mistake about it. Now, we should say that a physician who confused a matter of this sort was a cruel bungler if he did it carelessly, and a monster of malice if he did it purposely. One-half of the benefit of such a prophylactic, we should say, is in the sense of security which it gives to the minds of those who resort to it. The value of a course of treatment which is so uncertainly prescribed that no one can be sure whether he is following it, or not, would be very doubtful.

Now, the Great Physician has published a remedy for the plague of sin,—remedy and preventive in one; and can we suppose that he is either so careless, or so cruel, as to make it impossible for us to determine whether we have succeeded in applying it? That is quite incredible. It must be that those who strive to follow Christ may have a reasonable assurance that they are walking in the right way.

The Christian life is sometimes represented as a vocation or calling. It is not difficult for an individual to know whether or not he has entered upon any other calling. Some, indeed, there are, who have no definite occupation; but if a man has chosen a life-work, and devoted himself to it, he generally knows it. Ask him what his business is, and he will answer promptly enough, "I am a carpenter," or, "I am lawyer," or, "I am a druggist," or, "I am a machinist," as the case may be. The carpenter does not say to you, in a sad, uncertain tone of voice, "I don't know: I have been trying for five, or ten, or forty years, to be a carpenter, and I have sometimes hoped that I was one; indeed, there have been seasons when I felt quite sure of it; but I am often in great doubt." He may say, indeed, "I am not so good a carpenter as I might be; I have seen nicer workmen; but I can do a pretty fair job, and I am not ashamed of my trade. It is one that I freely chose, and that I have done my best to learn; and I shall work at it as long as I live, if I can find employment." Surely there is nothing presumptuous in saying as much as that. A man who did not have his mind made up about such a matter, and who did not know his own mind, would never accomplish much in this world.

And, if he were only an apprentice, he might confidently say, "I am going to be a carpenter if I live: I have chosen that as my life-work, and am learning it as fast as I can. I shall know the business better by and by, but I am working at it now every day."

How shall I know whether I am a Christian, or not?

Why is it not possible for those who have chosen the Christian vocation, and have devoted their lives to it, to know that they have done so?

The Christian life is sometimes represented as citizenship in a kingdom, or as loyalty to a government. Every one of us knows whether he is a loyal citizen of the United States, or not. If any one should ask you, in your journeyings abroad, what your nationality was, what would your answer be? Would you say, "Really, I am not quite sure. I have lived in the United States all my life, and have voted and paid taxes there, and have sometimes hoped that I might be considered a citizen of that country; but I am troubled with a good many doubts about it"? Or would you simply say, "I am an American," and mean to cover by that claim not only your birthright citizenship, but also the free and loyal love that binds you to your native land?

Why should you not be just as sure that you are loyal to Christ's kingdom as that you are loyal to the government of your country?

The Christian life is, as we have seen, not only allegiance to a government, but devotion to a person. It begins with a surrender of the soul, in an entire and unfaltering trust, to Jesus Christ the Saviour. Love to him, faith in him, union with him, are its constant inspiration. Now, it is not difficult for any of us to tell whether, or not, we are cherishing a personal affection for those who are nearest us in this world. The dutiful child is in no doubt as to whether he loves his mother, or not. The parent does not need to stop and search his heart to see whether he can find any traces of affection for his child. Your chosen friend, your most intimate companion,—you know what your

45

feelings are toward him. Why should there be any more uncertainty in your mind concerning your love for Christ? You
have not seen him, but you may communicate with him every
day and every hour. The bodily form in which he appeared to
men is not with us, but "we have the mind of Christ." His
thoughts are not only recorded for us in the New Testament,
but they are given us by direct inspiration, whenever we open
our minds to receive them. His love was not only manifested
to us on the cross, but it is revealed to us every day in care
the most constant, help the most loving, comfort the most sweet
and precious. The fact that we cannot see him is no reason why
we should not know him. Very likely there are persons in
this world, whom you have never seen, for whom you have con-
ceived a strong affection. You have been in communication
with them; their thoughts and feelings have been made known
to you; and, though you have not seen their faces or touched
their hands, you know their minds; and all love that is genuine
has a great deal more to do with the mind than with the face or
the hands. Now, communication with Christ is much more
direct, and may be much more constant, than with any earthly
friend, far or near; and there is no reason why our affection for
him should not constantly deepen and strengthen, no reason
why we should not be quite as sure that we love him as that we
love any other friend. For the faculties of the soul which are
called into exercise in loving him are the same faculties which
we exercise when we love our children or our parents or our
companions; and there is no more mystery in their use in the
one case than in the other.

The Christian life may also be considered as a hungering
and thirsting for righteousness. This, as we have seen, is the
principle from which it starts, and the goal toward which it

travels. You go to Christ because you hate sin, and desire to overcome it. You follow Christ because he promises to enable you to make his righteousness your own. Now, you know, of a certainty, whether or not this is your purpose. You know whether you have set before yourself righteousness, rather than happiness, as your being's end and aim. If this is the ruling motive of your life; if you want to be pure and true and good more than you want any thing else, and if by Christ's grace you mean to be, then you are a Christian. And there is no more difficulty in your knowing that this is your purpose, than in knowing that you have decided to buy a house, or to make a journey, or to study a profession.

Now, take these illustrations, and apply them to your own cases.

1. Have you chosen the service of Christ as your high calling, your life-work, with an honest intention of continuing in it, by his grace, as long as you shall live?

2. Are you loyal to his government? Is he the Lord of your life, the sovereign of your heart? Is it your sincere endeavor to seek first his kingdom?

3. Are you bound to him as to a friend, by a strong personal affection?

4. Are you striving with all your might to follow him in the way of righteousness?

If you are genuine disciples of Christ, I know that you will answer all of these questions promptly, unless it be the third one. Some of us may be able to respond to that with equal promptness. Doubtless all of us ought to be. But there are many Christians who hesitate when they are asked whether they are conscious of a personal affection for Christ. They know that they honor him, that they are grateful to him, and that they are trying to do his will; but they cannot speak, as some do, of that glowing love which unites the soul with Christ in a sweet consciousness of fellowship. This experience is one to which Christians do not always attain at the beginning of their course, but it is not beyond the reach of any of us; and a faithful following of Christ ought to lead us into it. Some persons are naturally more trustful than others, make friends more readily, respond more quickly to overtures of affection: such natures will more easily establish this personal relation with Christ, and will enter into *a feeling of union with him* more speedily, though they may be no more devout and no more devoted than some who cannot speak with confidence of any such experience.

But, even though in this respect your evidence that you are a Christian may not be so clear as you could wish, if you can answer the other three questions in the affirmative, you ought to know that you are a Christian. If you know that you have consecrated your life to the service of Christ, that you are loyal to his kingdom in purpose and in deed, and that you are endeavoring by his grace to walk in the way of righteousness, then you have no right to doubt that you are a Christian. For, if you know that these things are true of you, God knows it too, does he not? And, if he knows that such are your sincere desires and your honest endeavors, then, although you may make a great many mistakes, and may often fail of realizing your purposes, he will be patient and pitiful in his treatment of you; and he assures us that those whose hearts are turned toward him with such earnest purpose, he will in no wise cast out.

## How shall I know whether I am a Christian, or not?

*When you know that you have done, so far as you can, what is necessary in order to become a Christian, then you ought to know that you are a Christian.*

"God is not a man, that he should lie." He says to you, "Seek, and ye shall find." When, therefore, you know that you have earnestly sought, you know, if his word is true, that you have also found. To entertain any doubt of it, is to make him a liar. Though you may not have any evidence in your feelings that he accepts you as his child, you have his word for it; and you ought to have a great deal more confidence in his word than in the report of your own emotions.

"All this may be true," says some one, "but how can I be sure that I have earnestly sought him? May I not be deceived right here? May I not think that I am in earnest when I am not?"

No: I do not think that any one is ever deceived in this matter who does not want to be. You are dealing with a Being of perfect truth; and he would not suffer you to be innocently misled to your own ruin. If you are a deliberate hypocrite, then doubtless in deceiving others you may succeed in deceiving yourself; but, if you want to know the truth about your own spiritual condition, God's Spirit will reveal it to you. You are not self-deceived unless you are a wilful and conscienceless deceiver of others. And, if you honestly think that you have done what you could to become a Christian, you have no right to doubt that you are a Christian.

Every one of us may know what is the ruling purpose of his life; and he who knows that his ruling purpose is to trust and follow Christ knows that he is a Christian.

But there is another kind of evidence that is still more clear and satisfactory: that is the evidence which is furnished by the course of our own experience. By this, I do not mean the revelation which is made in consciousness. There are those who speak of an inner light,—a *feeling* of assurance, which is so strong that they rest their faith upon it. This is what Paul means, I suppose, by the witness of the Spirit; and those who have received it ought to be thankful for it. But there are Christians who cannot speak with confidence of any such evidence as this, who yet feel that they have in their own experience the most conclusive proofs that they are the children of God. Their confidence is not in any revelations which have been made to them, not in any light which they have seen, not in any ecstasy which they have felt. The ground of their hope is something much more commonplace, and much more stable. It is the whole history of their Christian lives.

They have been faithfully trying for years to reduce their religion to practice; and the proofs that their religion is true and real have been multiplying and strengthening, the longer they have lived. They have asked again and again for spiritual gifts from God, and have received what they asked for. They have been struggling against their faults and failings, trusting in the divine aid; and in this conflict they are sure that the help of the Omnipotent has been freely given to them. Vices and weaknesses which they never could overcome in their own strength, they have conquered by the grace of God. They can connect their prayers with these moral victories, as closely as they can connect any other cause with its effects.

So, too, in the work they have undertaken for others, it seems to them certain that they have had the help of the Master again and again. Duties from which they shrunk have been made easy; burdens which they thought would crush them have been wonderfully lightened; in the hour when their testimony was wanted, their tongues have been loosened; their timidity has been changed to courage, their doubt to confidence, their weakness to strength, by trusting in the divine Helper. They have proved God, and have found by long experience that the promises of his word are verities.

Their realization of the divine aid has been at some seasons much less vivid than at others. There have, indeed, been periods in their lives when they have neglected this close connection with the Power unseen; but the assurance of his ability to help has been exactly proportioned to the constancy and earnestness with which they have sought his aid. And, looking back over their history, they feel that the proof of the reality of the Christian life is cumulative,—that it rests not wholly upon the assurance of another, but largely upon experience; and that it is in great measure the kind of proof which scientific men insist upon,—an induction of facts which have come within their own knowledge.

This is a conviction into which every man must make his own way. Every one of us must give account for himself unto God, and every one of us must find out for himself whether God's word is true. The religious experience is wholly individual. It is impossible for us to reach and tabulate the facts of other men's lives, because it is impossible for us to know what the mental experiences of other men are. We know what takes place in our own minds, but we cannot tell what is passing in the minds of others.

It will be observed, too, that this conviction of the truths of religion is the result neither of metaphysics nor of mysticism,

51

but that it is produced by a steady and patient endeavor to reduce Christianity to life. If you want to know the certainty of these things, you must put them in practice. If you wish to find out whether a machine will work, you set it a-going. If you want to know whether a coat will fit, you put it on. The religion of Christ is a practical religion ; and the only test which you can apply to it is the test of use. If you will take the Master at his word, and do his will, you shall know of the doctrine ; not merely by the shining of an inner light, nor by the deductions of a halting logic, but by the solid persuasion which grows out of a happy and fruitful life.

But some one wants to know whether in becoming a Christian one does not experience a change of heart, and whether one can experience such a change without knowing it immediately.

Certainly, I answer : a change of heart does take place when one becomes a Christian. "Ye must be born again," the Saviour said to Nicodemus ; and he who consecrates himself to the service of Christ, who learns of him and follows him, does experience the regenerating grace of God. But I do not think that men are always conscious of this change when it takes place. All analogy is against such a theory. The beginnings of life are always small and silent. Were you conscious of the beginning of your natural life? Do you even remember the first moment of your consciousness? No : you had been breathing, and thinking, and wondering, and wishing, and suffering, and taking pleasure, for weeks and months before anything happened which you can remember. And it is very often that the new life begins in just this way. You are conscious of your own resolutions, your own struggles, your own attempts by faith to lay hold upon eternal life ; but the operations of the

Divine Spirit go on in your heart for a long time beneath consciousness, and the change that is wrought in you is wrought without noise or demonstration.

This phrase, "a change of heart," is one over which beginners in the Christian life are wont to stumble. It seems to them to suggest an emotional experience so marked and distinct, that they shall know when they have passed through it; and, since they do not have any such experience, they begin to doubt whether they have become Christians.

I knew a young man, more than twenty years ago, who found himself in just this perplexity. He had been trying for several weeks to live a Christian life, doing every duty as well as he knew how, and praying all the while for light and help; but still he failed to experience what he expected; and he went to his pastor, and sadly told him that there was something wrong.

"What is the trouble?" asked the minister. "I thought you were getting on bravely. Are you growing weary in your service?"

"Oh, no! but I haven't met with a change of heart. I thought that I should, if I kept trusting Christ, and trying to do his will, but I haven't."

"How do you know that you haven't?"

"Well, it seems to me that I should have known, if I had."

"Would you? Perhaps not. Let us see. You have not experienced a change of heart. What is the heart?"

"The affections, I suppose."

"Exactly. Now, are you sure that your affections have not changed? Did you love to read the Bible six weeks ago?"

"No."

53

"Do you now?"

"I do."

"Did you love to pray before that time?"

"No: I said my prayers generally; but I didn't pray much."

"Do you find pleasure in your prayers now, as well as profit?"

"Oh, yes!"

"Did you enjoy going to prayer-meeting or talking with Christians about religion six weeks ago?"

"Not at all."

"And you do now?"

"I do, very much."

"You can think, can you not, of several things, that you *did* find pleasure in not long ago, in which you find no pleasure now?"

"Yes: a good many."

"Well, then," said the minister, "I should think that you had met with a great change of heart. That which you loved most a short time ago, you care but little for now; that which you cared nothing for then is your chief enjoyment now. It seems to me that your affections have almost wholly changed; and, if by the heart is meant the affections, you have certainly experienced a change of heart."

That young man will never cease to be grateful to his minister for taking this phrase, which had been a barrier before his feet, and turning it into a staff to help him on his way. It is possible that the report of this simple conversation might make the way of life plainer for some of you.

## Chapter V

## When should I join the Church?

"THAT is not the first question," says somebody. "The first question is whether there is any need of joining the church at all. Cannot one be a Christian outside the church as well as inside?"

I have no doubt that one can be a Christian without joining the church. There is no salvation in the sacraments, and there is no regenerating virtue in religious professions. But I do not think that you can be so good a Christian outside the church as you can be inside. You are not so good a Christian when you are neglecting a plain duty as you are when you are performing it. And joining the church is a plain duty for all who mean to be Christians.

Can there be any doubt about this? Do not the explicit commands of our Saviour put this matter quite beyond the reach of question or cavil?

"Whosoever therefore shall confess me before men, him will I confess also before my Father which is in heaven; but whosoever shall deny me before men, him will I also deny before my Father which is in heaven."

These are plain words, and they are solemn words. It is vain to try to explain them away, or to evade their application. They mean just what they say; and they make it the duty of every one who recognizes Christ as his Lord and Master, to make a public profession of his faith in him.

Does any one doubt that Christ founded a church in the world into which men were to be received by baptism? Does any one forget that his last word to his followers was, "Go ye and disciple all nations, baptizing them in the name of the Father, and of the Son, and of the Holy Ghost"? Telling them to baptize everybody is certainly equivalent to telling everybody to be baptized by them. It is no more true that God commands all men everywhere to repent, than that Christ commands all men everywhere to be baptized.

The Lord's Supper is the other sacrament of the church. And the observance of this is not only a sacred privilege but a solemn duty. "*Do this* in remembrance of me." It is not only an invitation, it is also a command. You cannot claim that you are obeying him so long as you neglect this clear and explicit injunction which was spoken by his own lips.

I said that one could doubtless be a Christian without joining the church; but that is only saying that one may be a Christian who neglects a plain duty. For there are some Christians who are so blinded by prejudice or error, that they refuse to perform the plainest duties. There can be no doubt, for example, that it is the duty of every citizen of this government to take part in the government, by informing himself concerning the issues that are pending, and by casting his vote, in every election, for the best policy and the best candidates. It is not only a political duty, it is a Christian duty; for Christ bids us "render to Cæsar the things that are Cæsar's." Moreover, Paul tells us that "the powers that be are ordained of God," not to bear the sword in vain, but to do justice and judgment; and in this country the people are "the powers that be," the sovereign authority, upon whom the responsibilities of government are laid. Yet there are Christians who neglect this plain duty, and some who even refuse to perform it, holding themselves entirely aloof from politics, because the government is, in their view, defective in its form, or because there are so many evils in its administration. Now, it seems plain, doubtless, to all of us, that such conduct as this is not only foolish but inexcusable. If the government is not what it ought to be, it is every citizen's duty to do what he can by voice and vote to make it better. A man who neglects this duty may be a Christian, but he is not so good a Christian as he would be if he performed it.

The duty of taking part in the government of the state is much less urgent than the duty of taking part in the work of the church. Political governments are imperfect and short-lived, and there is no promise of the continuance of any of them.

> "Our little systems have their day,—
> They have their day, and cease to be;"

But the church endures from generation to generation: it is the one kingdom that cannot be moved; it is the one instrumentality which is divinely ordained and indestructible; and the work of God in the world is carried on in it and by means of it. In spite of all the imperfections and corruptions which must attach to anything in which men are engaged, the church is manifestly under the control of the divine wisdom; it is the means which God has chosen for the salvation of men. To say, therefore, that you are not under obligation to connect yourself with it, and to give it your loyal support, is to impugn God's wisdom, to say that you know a better way of saving the world than the way that he has chosen. The refusal to enter its ranks, and do what you can to increase its victorious

57

strength, is unfaithfulness of the same kind as that of the citizen who holds himself aloof from all political action; nay, as much worse than his as the church is higher and diviner than the state.

The reasons urged upon you for joining the church are often reasons which appeal to your self-interest. You are told that it will help you in living a Christian life; that the ordinances and the fellowship of the church give stimulus and strength to those who walk in them; that, if you do not thus identify yourself with God's people, you will be likely to lose your interest in religion, and to drift away into utter worldliness. And these words are true, beyond a doubt. I have seen them proved true a great many times. You ought not to lose sight of these considerations; but, after all, the strong reason for joining the church is not that you will gain by it, but that it is your duty to do it. No command of Christ is more express. No duty is further removed from the sphere of casuistry. It is a matter concerning which those who have chosen Christ for their master cannot stop to argue.

If, then, it is a plain duty to join the church, the question which we set out to answer is answered already. The time to do any plain duty is the present time, or the earliest possible time. It is my duty to speak the truth. When shall I speak the truth? Now, every day, continually. It is my duty to deal honestly. When? Whenever I have any dealings. It is my duty to make reparation to my neighbor of any wrong that I have done him. When? Just as soon as I am able to do it. Not when I feel like it, not when it is convenient to do it; but, setting aside all considerations of pleasure or convenience, just as speedily as I may.

## When should I join the Church?

It is my duty to make a public profession of my faith in Christ, and connect myself with his church. When? At the very first opportunity. There is no more warrant for delay than there is in the presence of any other clear obligation.

When the citizen comes of age, you never hear him asking when he shall begin to vote. He votes, if he is an intelligent and conscientious man, at the first election, and at every succeeding election when it is within his power. He begins to exercise the duties of citizenship as soon as he becomes a citizen. He sees to it that his name is enrolled on the registry lists, that he may be counted among the responsible electors and rulers of the land. What would you think of the man who neglected this duty because he did not feel patriotic or public-spirited enough to perform it; who kept waiting, year by year, till he should feel that he was a good citizen, before he began to do his duty as a citizen? Would you not tell him that the way to become a good citizen was by performing, rather than neglecting, the most obvious duties of citizenship?

But this is just the excuse which is given for not joining the church, by many of those who confess that they have chosen the service of Christ, and that they are endeavoring to live as Christians. They are not good enough, they say. And you think, do you, good friends, that you will become better Christians by refusing to obey the express command of Christ? How long do you think it will take you, walking in this path of disobedience, trampling his most positive orders under your feet every day, to reach that perfection of character which shall fit you for membership in his church?

But you are not disobedient, you say, at least not consciously and deliberately, to any command but this. You are earnestly

59

trying to live a Christian life, to overcome your sins, and to grow in all the graces of the Christian character. This is the only duty that you wilfully neglect.

I am glad to believe that this is true of some of you: yet who gave you permission to neglect one plain duty? Where did you get your dispensation of disobedience in this one thing? Does not the Christian law of consecration call for the whole heart? Is not this keeping back of part of the price the very essence of unbelief? Do we not read that he who keeps the whole law, and yet offends in one point, the same is guilty of all? This halting submission, which stops just short of full obedience, is not what Christ expects of his followers.

But you protest that your only reason for refusing to confess your faith in Christ is that you are not good enough. If you were good enough, there would be no need of confessing Christ,—no need of Christ at all. It is just because you are not good enough, that Christ says to you, "Follow me." He came not to call the righteous, but sinners, to repentance. It is not the perfect people, or the self-satisfied people, whom he wants in his church, but those who have a deep sense of their own imperfection, and who believe that his strength is made perfect in weakness.

What is more, your expectation that you will "grow better in staying away,"—better in your own sight,—is one that will not be fulfilled. It is just as true of joining the church as it is of becoming a Christian, that, if you tarry till you feel that you are better, you will never come at all.

How many I have known who have tried this experiment faithfully, and have found out the folly of it! A lady once came to me, desiring to unite with the church. I asked her how long she had been a Christian; and she told me that she gave herself to the service of Christ more than twenty years ago.

"Have you been faithfully trying to live as a Christian all these years?" I asked.

"I have," was the answer.

"Why, then, have you not before this time made a profession of your faith?"

"Because I wanted to be better satisfied with my religious experience," she replied. "I did not feel that I was good enough to join the church; and I wanted to wait till I was better."

"And do you feel that you are better now?"

"No: I do not" (very positively). "I am not any better satisfied with myself than I was when I began to follow Christ. I see my own imperfections quite as clearly as I did then. But I have made up my mind that it is my duty to confess my faith in the Saviour who died for me; and I know that, if I wait till I am satisfied with my own condition, I shall wait forever."

That is only one of many testimonies to the same effect that I have heard from the lips of those who had been waiting until they were worthy to join the church. I never heard anybody say that he was glad that he had waited. I never heard anybody express the opinion, at the end of a period of waiting, that he was worthier to be a church-member than he was when he first entered upon the Christian course. I have heard almost uniformly, from such persons, regrets that the public confession had not been more promptly made.

"Was it true, then," you ask, "that these persons had grown no better through all these months and years of waiting? How can a person be a Christian, and not improve in character? Are we not often told that that is just what is meant by being a Christian?"

To this I answer, that it is not necessary to suppose that these persons had made no progress at all. They had not advanced as rapidly as they ought to have done, because one who neglects an obvious duty must, by that very neglect, be crippled in the Christian race. The thought of his disobedience is a weight about his neck. But the fact is, that one is not conscious of progress in the Christian life. He may know that his prayers are answered; he may be certain that he has help from on high in overcoming his sins; but he is all the while discovering his limitations and his weaknesses; all the while finding new battles to fight, and new heights to climb; and, *so far as his own feeling of worthiness is concerned,* that does not become any more assured and satisfying as the time goes by. His growth in grace, if he makes any growth, is accompanied by a constant elevation of his standard of living. His ideals go before him, and they travel as fast as he does. You may fix your eyes on the brightest constellation in the firmament, and follow it round the world without coming any nearer it. No charm is given to your fidelity "to stay the morning star in his steep course." The beauty of the rainbow is always just so far in advance of your feet. Between what you are, and what you ought to be, the disparity, so far as your own feelings are concerned, is never lessened by your continuance in well-doing. When, therefore, you wait until you shall feel more worthy to be a member of Christ's church, you wait for what, in the nature of the case, you can never attain, unless, indeed, you become a self-righteous hypocrite.

But you say that you are delaying because you are afraid that if you join the church you may bring discredit upon the cause of Christ. Many professors of religion do, by their inconsistent lives, put the church to shame. You hear them spoken of as stumbling-blocks; you see that the logic of their lives tends to confute, rather than to confirm, the holy gospel they profess; and you do not want to be numbered among them. God forbid that you should be! But is there any need that you should be? Have you not committed your soul to Him who is able to keep you from falling, and do you not believe that he will do it? Everyone that is God's faithful servant shall surely be holden up, for God is able to make him stand. That is his word; do you not believe that it is true? If you have intrusted yourself to Christ, and are living by faith in him; if you have surrendered yourself to his service and his guidance and his keeping, then your distrust of being able to live an upright and consistent life is distrust of him, not of yourself. It is an accusation of unfaithfulness brought against him. It is a confession of your doubt either of his power, or of his truthfulness. You do not wish to admit that you are harboring any such doubt as that!

But consider, pray, whether you are not, by refusing or delaying to identify yourself with Christ and his church, doing what you can, even now, to bring discredit upon his cause. You are saying in effect that his establishment in the world, of a visible church, was a superfluous work; that the world would be just as well off without the church as with it; that the maintenance of its organization is a matter of no importance. More than that, you are saying that men have a perfect right to pick and choose among the commands of Christ; obeying such of them as are convenient, and disregarding the rest. "Repent, and be baptized, every one of you," is the divine order. "No," you say; "everybody ought to repent, of course; but only those should be baptized and join the church who feel like it. That is not a matter of obligation." Your lives are saying just that. No matter how many disclaimers you may put in, that is what your actions mean; and it is by your actions that you are judged. I see not how you could bring discredit upon Christ and his gospel more effectually than by this preemptory refusal to obey his plain command.

Remember, my friends, that you are counted on the one side or on the other. "He that is not with me is against me," the Master says. If you will not be numbered among his friends, you are sure to be numbered among those who are not his friends. That is a category in which you do not desire to be put.

There are some among you, who have long been endeavoring in a secret and somewhat unsteady fashion to lead a Christian life. You are not at all satisfied with the progress you have made, and you have a great many doubts about yourselves; but you are nevertheless trying to trust in the Saviour, and to follow him. The expectation of being at some time in your lives pronounced and positive disciples of Christ is one that you constantly cherish; nothing could induce you to abandon it. Is it not a good time now to forsake your concealed and equivocal position, and come right to the front? Do you not want to make your lives tell decisively and powerfully on the side of truth and goodness from this day onward? And is not the cause of Christ in the world the cause of truth and goodness? Would not the triumph of his gospel be the triumph of all that is highest and holiest? Notwithstanding the imperfections of the church, and the inconsistencies of its members, all of which I see as clearly as you do and lament as deeply, are not the best interests of all our communities bound up with the churches? And, if mischiefs do abound in them, is it not therefore the right and manly thing, not to stand apart carping and sneering, but to take hold of them vigorously, and in the strength of God endeavor to make them better? Would you not feel better satisfied with yourself if you were giving your lives zealously and effectively to this highest of all labors? Are you not conscious that you are defrauding yourself of a most precious right and privilege when you refuse to take an active part in Christ's work?

Answer these questions, my friends, at the bar of your own consciences, and remember that you must answer them one day before a more august tribunal. For the matter which we are considering is not a matter of convenience or expediency: it is a matter of duty. By the express command of Him whom you call Master, the obligation is laid upon you. The obligation will become a privilege, as every duty does which he gives us to do, if we only take it up cheerfully and discharge it faithfully; but it is none the less an obligation. And let us beware how we seek to evade or to defer so plain a duty.

## Chapter VI

## But and If

WHEN we dig down through the layers of indifference and hostility under which men often keep their consciences covered from the appeals of God's word, we sometimes strike into what may be called the butandiferous formati. It is a conglomerate of objections and excuses; and, like the Pennsylvanian coal measures, it is practically inexhaustible. The "buts" and the "ifs" which are unearthed by every exploration into the consciousness of those who refuse to enter upon the religious life are as many and as various as the fossils in the palæozoic rocks. We have encountered several of them already in the course of these conversations; but there are a few more left, of which we may well take notice.

"I should be ready to enter upon the Christian life," says one who comes clad in the garb of a philosopher, "if it did not demand of me the abdication of my manhood. You tell me that I must intrust myself to Christ; that I must submit to be instructed and guided and helped by him; that my will must be merged in his. But this is what no man must do. No man should submit his will to the dictation of any power outside of himself. Every man must be the arbiter of his own conduct. The humility and dependence which the religion of Christ enjoins are inconsistent with true manhood."

Your objection is a radical one, my friend philosopher, and it is not an uncommon one. In one form or another it is often urged. Mr. Mill tells us, that what we want in this world, or at any rate in some parts of it, is less of Christian self-denial, and more of Pagan self-assertion. Of that part of the world which Mr. Mill inhabited, this may be true; but it does not seem to me to hold good of regions hereabout. Yet even here there are voices which give forth the same sound; and the method of our religion which requires the subordination of the heart to a Master, of the life to a Ruler, is attacked as being unsound and unmanly.

Nevertheless the necessity of submission and dependence is pretty clearly established without going to the New Testament to seek its foundations. Lordly and self-reliant as man is, he is yet constantly compelled to submit. Water will run down hill, let him will the contrary however stoutly. His firmest resolutions and his most vigorous endeavors are inadequate to keep the sun above the horizon a moment beyond its time of setting. The tides will ebb and flow in spite of him; the rain and the snow fall many times quite against his will; the storm drives his ship upon the breakers without asking his consent; the thunderbolt shatters his dwelling, and he cannot help himself. All he can do is to submit. If he does it gracefully, so much the better for him: if he chafes and struggles, it makes no difference whatever with the storms or the tides or the currents or the planets. Man is surrounded on all sides with barriers which he cannot transgress. He may beat his life out against them, but he cannot overthrow them. They will confine him, and he must yield to them.

He is obliged not only to submit, but also to depend. He must depend upon the sun and the showers for his crops; he must depend upon the air he breathes for life; he must depend upon the laws and forces of Nature for all his operations. He is all the while dependent.

Now, is it not quite absurd for a creature subject to so many limitations, compelled to submit to superior power and to depend upon superior strength every moment of his life, to set himself up and say, "I will not submit. I will not depend. It is cowardly to submit. It is weak and unmanly to depend"? That is a false theory of life which rests upon such foundations.

Before Lord Bacon's day, philosophy had been led.perpetually in a mad dance after all manner of vagaries. The sages had adopted just your method, my friend objector. They had said, "Man is the lord of creation: it belongs to him to lay down the laws of creation." So they had been sitting still in their libraries, and fashioning elaborate theories of natural law, and then going forth to hang their theories upon the facts. But somehow the theories would never fit the facts. So philosophy was, in great part, a wild jumble of contradictions with very little certainty or coherency.

But Bacon set out with a different method. His maxim was that man is the interpreter, rather than the lord, of Nature; and he urged that we must sit down submissively at her feet, and observe her operations and her processes, from our observation inferring the truths of science. The result is, that we have now certainty and system in science, where before all was blank confusion. This method of submissive study substituted for the method of proud theorizing has brought order out of chaos, and light out of darkness.

The right method in philosophy is the right method in all departments of life Bacon himself testified that the entrance to the temple of philosophy was exactly like the entrance to the temple of religion. Each is a strait gate, a humble portal. No man can go in at either without stooping and divesting himself of egotism and haughtiness. "Except ye be converted and become as little children ye can in no case enter therein," is as true of the one as of the other.

Therefore, when you tell me, my friend, that this humble submission and dependence which the religion of Christ requires of you is unreasonable and unmanly, I shall answer that, in the opinion of the greatest philosophers of our Anglo-Saxon race, it is the highest reason and the noblest manliness. The wisest men are always the humblest, the most willing to be led by truth, the most easy to be entreated. To yield to the demands of right is not unmanly. You abdicate your manhood not when you submit to the claims of righteousness, but when you refuse to do it. And he who submits to Christ submits only to truth and right; not to an arbitrary and unreasoning ruler, but to One whose law is perfect, and whose counsels are infallible.

I hear another objection which goes to the foundations of our Christianity. "There are many sound maxims in Christian ethics," says the critic; "but the command to love our neighbor as ourselves is unreasonable. Reason teaches us to take care of ourselves. Self-preservation, not self-denial, is the first law of nature."

But answer me, my friend, do you not admire most the persons who set that law at nought? When you see one man perilling his life to rescue another, dying to save another, is there not something within you which cries out in heartiest applause? The heroes of all patriotic warfare,—the men who give their lives for liberty and fatherland,—do not they disobey that law of self-preservation? and does not your very soul shout acclamations in their praise because they disobey it, because they count not their lives dear unto them, so that they may leave their country whole and free to posterity? Is there not a voice of your spirits which always commends self-sacrifice; which always condemns, in no measured cadences, every thing which looks like selfish forgetfulness of the welfare of others?

"Ah, yes," you reply, "but that is impulse; that is not reason. When I sit coolly down and reason about it, I reach the conclusion that each one has enough to do to attend to his own affairs, without troubling himself with the necessities of his fellows."

My friend, these utterances of your spirit which you call impulses are simply moral intuitions. They are the highest forms of reason. If you fall into the habit of disregarding them, or coolly sitting down and dissecting them, you inflict a death-wound upon your moral nature. When you arrive at the condition in which you never do anything from impulse, you have got about as low as you can go. When that voice within your heart is silenced, which thunders forth its anathemas at meanness and selfish greed, and rings out its peals of approbation in the presence of heroic self-denial, the very light that is in you will be darkness. Logic is lame; it arrives at its conclusions tardily, it often goes by the wrong road, and it sometimes gets to the wrong place. But this prompter that speaks from your moral intuitions, this faculty that, without stopping to debate, says quickly of an action, "It is right," or "It is wrong,"—this you must not doubt. And it is this faculty which says instantly, whenever we see this law of love to our neighbor obeyed, "It is right." This law bears the same relation to morals that the axioms bear to mathematics. I cannot prove by reasoning, though I know by reason, that two times two is four. I cannot prove by reasoning, but I know by reason, that it is right for us to love our neighbors as ourselves. All the logic in the world cannot convince me, nor you either, my friend, that it is not right.

Another objector declares that the doctrines of our religion are not credible. "I cannot accept the statements you make," he says, "because they are essentially mysterious. There is nothing like them within the range of my experience. It is impossible for me to verify them; you must not ask me to say that I believe any thing which I cannot verify."

I know that some truths are revealed in the Bible which cannot be explained. They are truths which relate to God, to the mode of his existence, to the methods by which he has made himself known to men. But is it not, to begin with, rational to suppose that any revelation of God will contain some things which will be difficult of comprehension? *That* the Infinite is, reason clearly tells us; *what* the Infinite is, reason can never fully comprehend. Infinite Being is too large for our categories; the thought cannot reach round it, and describe it; all attempts to make its substance known to us must be tentative and experimental. If there was nothing in the Bible about God which was not perfectly clear and intelligible; if no paths were opened to our thought, whose end we could not quickly reach,—it would be impossible for us to believe the Bible to be a revelation from an Infinite Being  The shadows of mystery which lie upon its pages are proofs of its divine origin.

But it is not only in our religion, my friend, that you find mysteries. Many things, just as hard to comprehend and explain, confront you every day in the creatures with which both kingdoms of life are teeming. I can ask you as many hard questions about a daisy or an oyster, as you can ask me about the God of the Bible. The mystery of life is absolutely insoluble by all your science,—always has been, always will be.

> "Flower in the crannied wall,
>   I pluck you out of the crannies;
>   Hold you here, root and all, in my hand,
>   Little flower; but if I could understand
>   What you are, root and all, and all in all,
>   I should know what God and man is."

You cannot understand the doctrine of the incarnation,— how God could become man. But you believe, I suppose, that God exists, that he is perfect and infinite, and that he is the Creator of the heavens and the earth. Explain to me, if you can, how an infinitely perfect being could ever have created any thing. Listen to Origen: "If to create is agreeable to the divine essence, how is it conceivable, that what is thus conformable to God's nature should at any time have been wanting?" The things that are made are not eternal: they once began to be. "There was a period, then, during which God was not creating any thing: an eternity had passed before he began to create. But a transition from a state of not-creating to the act of creation is inconceivable without a change," and God is unchangeable. It is beyond the power of man to conceive of the creation of the universe by an infinitely perfect being. It is not unreasonable, but it is inconceivable. There is nothing like it in your experience, and of course you cannot verify it. The whole subject is environed with mysteries and contradictions, yet you do not relinquish your belief that the universe was created: and you cannot relinquish it without running against difficulties equally formidable, whether you turn toward atheism or pantheism. There are just as many inconceivabilities in atheism and in pantheism as in theism.

To reject the gospel on account of the mysteries which it contains, and yet hold fast to other beliefs which are equally mysterious, is a palpable inconsistency.

You complain that some things are revealed which you cannot verify. That is true. But some things are told you which you can verify. There are mysteries in theological science, as there are mysteries in physiological science; but there are plain principles laid down in each of these sciences which you can test for yourselves. Physiology says that good bread, if it is eaten, will support life. You may not understand all the mysteries of digestion and assimilation, but you can verify that statement. The New Testament says that faith in the Lord Jesus Christ will save the soul from sin. You may not comprehend all the mysteries of the incarnation and the atonement; but here is the one truth which concerns you, and you can verify it. You can find out, of a certainty, whether he is able to deliver you from the evil, and to strengthen you in righteousness. "It is so," says Matthew Arnold: "try it, and you will find it to be so. Try all the ways to righteousness that you can think of, and you will find that no way brings you to it except the way of Jesus, but that this way does bring you to it." This is the test to which our religion is always ready to submit. This is the test which the Lord himself has appointed. He has not promised that the universe shall contain no mysteries; he could not promise that without taking himself out of the universe: but he does promise, that if we will trust him, and obey him, he will give us power to overcome the evil,— power to become the sons of God. And the man who refuses to put that promise to the proof most clearly shows that his mind is not in a condition to receive any vital truth.

A host of these objections and excuses yet remain, which I must dismiss with only a word of argument.

"I suppose," says one, "that these things are true; but I cannot realize their truth. The whole subject of religion is to me hazy and unreal." Of course it is; and it always will be until you have applied it to your own life. You cannot realize that honey is sweet until you have tasted it. "Taste, and see that the Lord is good." You cannot realize the luxury of doing good till you have tried it. The substance of all realities is in this religion of Jesus Christ; but it can be real only to those who will do his will.

"But, if I am of the number of the elect, I shall be saved at any rate; and, if I am not of that number, it is no use for me to try to save myself." Now, my friend, you either believe this doctrine of election, or you don't believe it. If you don't believe it, you have no right to quote it as an excuse. If you do believe it, you believe that God has foreordained all things, whatsoever comes to pass. His decrees determine every other department of your life, as well as your religious experience. If it is decreed that you shall be rich, you will be rich; and, according to your logic, there is no need that you should turn over your hand to increase your store. If it is decreed that you should build a house, or harvest a crop, or make a journey, or understand a science, all these things will come to pass. You may sit still, and fold your hands, and, whatever God has appointed for you, you will be sure to get. But you do not act on that principle in secular matters; and you would say that a man who did so was a fool. The practice would be just as rational in secular matters as it is in religious matters.

"But what can mortal man do to secure his own salvation?" (I am quoting the very words of a question that was addressed to me.) Mortal man can do just what God bids him do. He can repent and believe. He can arise and follow Christ, as Matthew did.

"I know that I ought to do it; but I can't decide." You can decide. "Choose ye whom ye will serve." The power of choice is yours. The responsibility of choice rests upon you, and upon you alone. God cannot choose for you. But you can settle the question, if you will, this very hour. You know that you can.

"But I want to act deliberately. I do not want to take this step rashly." Deliberately! How long have you been deliberating on this matter? All of you for many months, most of you for many years. Have you not taken time enough to deliberate? Let me tell you, my friend, it is not well to stop very long to think when a plain duty summons you. The sooner you do it, the better. Suppose that you have done your neighbor a wrong, and you are moved to go and confess it, and ask his pardon. "But wait," you say. "Let me not be rash about this. Let me take time to deliberate." So you sit down and think it over, and give the selfish passions of your soul time to assert themselves. You are able, perhaps, in your deliberation, to think of some unkindness that your neighbor has done you: at any rate, you can find flaws enough in his life; and very likely you may succeed in getting yourself into a frame of mind in which frank acknowledgment of the wrong you have done him will be altogether impossible. Deliberation upon a deed to which honor and magnanimity and all the nobler sentiments prompt you is too apt to strangle the impulse that leads you to do it. It is just such a deed as this which you now propose to ponder and discuss a little longer. My friend, you cannot afford to do it. You have hurt yourself already by your deliberation. The time to decide is now.